THE BEST OF ADRIAN RAESIDE

A TREASURY OF BC CARTOONS

··· A TREASURY OF BC CARTOONS ···

ADRIAN RAESIDE

THE BEST OF ADRIAN RAESIDE

HARBOUR PUBLISHING

1 2 3 4 5 — 18 17 16 15 14

Harbour Publishing Co. Ltd.
P.O. Box 219, Madeira Park, BC, V0N 2H0
www.harbourpublishing.com

Cover and text design by Teresa Karbashewski
Printed and bound in Canada

BRITISH COLUMBIA
ARTS COUNCIL
An agency of the Province of British Columbia

Canada Council   Conseil des Arts
for the Arts   du Canada

Harbour Publishing acknowledges financial support from the Government of Canada through the Canada Book Fund and the Canada Council for the Arts, and from the Province of British Columbia through the BC Arts Council and the Book Publishing Tax Credit.

Cataloguing data available from Library and Archives Canada
ISBN 978-1-55017-631-5 (paper)
ISBN 978-1-55017-633-9 (ebook)

For licencing and reprinting cartoons in this book contact adrian@raesidecartoon.com. For more Raeside cartoons go to www.raesidecartoon.com.

AMONG ALL THE PROVINCES, British Columbia is decidedly unique. Our premiers often leave office in disgrace, our public sector unions have perfected the fine art of hostage-taking, our environmentalists have perfected the fine art of chaining themselves to logging trucks (even when they're moving), our ferries charge outrageous fares (and then don't go anywhere), our hockey team never wins the Stanley Cup (but then, neither does Toronto's), we build elaborate houses few of us can afford, and we're suspicious of anything that comes from beyond the Rocky Mountains—specifically, anyone from Ottawa... or Alberta oil. The mountains also act as a cultural barrier, allowing us the freedom to get on with our gay weddings on skis, pot smoke-ins and group tree-hugs—assuming those events aren't disrupted by a mudslide, flood, forest fire or massive earthquake.

Over the last thirty-five years I've drawn roughly seven thousand cartoons on BC-specific topics—everything from aging ferries to Zalm—but could fit only about two hundred and thirty of them into this book. If I missed the cartoon on your favourite scandal from the past, I apologize. If, however, I have included a cartoon exposing a scandal that you were responsible for, please accept my sincere thanks for keeping me gainfully employed.

—Adrian Raeside

WE HAVE NO CLUE how to drive in snow—and we're proud of it. We'll happily queue for twenty minutes to get a chai latte but won't spend twenty seconds learning what a Single Transferable Vote is—and we're proud of it. We'll spend millions on installing bike lanes but will never give up our SUVs—and we're proud of it. (It's tough lugging your skis up to Whistler on a bike.) We hate ICBC and BC Hydro—but we'll lynch any politician who dares to float the idea of selling them. We're a province full of contradictions—and we're proud of it.

The BC coast experiences the rare snowfall—which would be fine if we just stayed home and built transgendered snowpersons.

Negotiations between the BC Teachers' Federation (BCTF) and the BC Public School Employers' Association are like one long, endless trip to the dentist.

In order to scrape up the down payment for a house in Vancouver, not only do you need to sell a kidney, but your parents and grandparents have to sell their kidneys too.

Or, you could just make a dash for it when they're reloading.

Yet another traditional resource-based industry is decimated in BC. Will there be a going-out-of-business sale?

When, in fact, it should be DFO officials in Ottawa who are decommissioned and auctioned off.

When the theft of copper wire reached epidemic proportions, scrap metal dealers were expected to question their suppliers.

These cars are in fact useless, as there is no room for a large dog.

Vancouver gets snazzy transit lines, the rest of the province gets potholes.

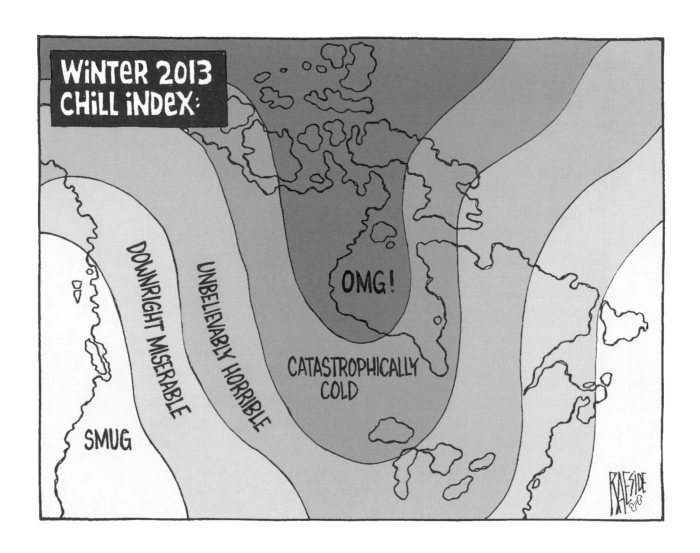

The most eagerly anticipated winter sport for coastal residents is phoning relatives back East when the first daffodil makes its appearance—in early February.

Kind of like building a solar-powered house next to a neighbour who heats their house by burning rubber tires.

Sneakers containing human feet were mysteriously washing ashore, stumping forensic scientists, when in fact there was a perfectly logical explanation.

Paving over agricultural land is no longer the exclusive domain of rich white developers.

Where he will commute to the city in a hydrocarbon-spewing SUV on a six-lane highway.

At one time the Vancouver skyline was dominated by blue tarpaulins, prompting some to suggest BC's provincial flower be changed from the Pacific dogwood to black mould.

Some homeowners, fearing electromagnetic radiation from digital smart meters, went to extraordinary lengths to prevent BC Hydro from replacing their old analog meters.

As one of the first provinces to legalize gay marriage, same-sex couples can now live as regular happily married couples.

Every ferry disruption revives the debate over constructing a bridge to the Gulf Islands—but a bridge could mean that the islands' real estate developers would be overwhelmed by mainland real estate developers.

BC banned adults from smoking in cars that they share with child passengers—but it's okay for everyone to suck in the exhaust from thousands of large trucks and buses.

British Columbia is known as the "morons-who-go-out-into-the-wilderness-completely-unprepared-and-have-to-get-rescued" capital of the world.

YOU'VE SEEN THE ADS: beauty shots of BC's natural wonders that tout this province as the place to live and play—natural wonders that won't be so wonderful if development continues at the current feverish pace. The Site C dam will submerge thousands of hectares of productive farmland, and Megamall parking lots are paving over what's left. Pristine rivers and streams are threatened by a proposed pipeline transporting Alberta's oil to BC's coast, oozing past gas fracking operations. From there, oil tankers will have to negotiate a rock-strewn waterway not much wider than a suburban ditch. And if one of those rocks should happen to get in the way of a tanker, the Coast Guard will be there to respond from the nearest Coast Guard station, which—due to budget cuts—will be stationed on the Rideau Canal in Ottawa.

Giant-screen TV: 1. Wildlife: 0.

And of course, we need a place to put our giant-screen TV.

Premier Mike Harcourt's NDP government went out of its way to placate its base.

Perhaps we could, if grocery wholesalers paid local farmers more for their produce.

CN, who bought BC Rail at a fire-sale price, couldn't seem to keep their trains on the rails. Instead, they were ending up in our fish-bearing streams and rivers.

Pesticides: Mother Nature's Chernobyl.

Although tasing it would be more environmentally friendly.

In British Columbia, what used to be wilderness is only a short drive away.

And when you get there, things aren't always as they used to be.

Contrary to the claims of Enbridge, builders of the Northern Gateway Pipeline, isolated incidents that hardly ever happen... keep happening.

Even Premier Christy Clark was against the Northern Gateway Pipeline...
sort of.

Sadly, it's not just oil pipelines that threaten our rivers and streams...

...and one by one our waterways may be lost forever.

* NOW DO IT IN THE MIDDLE OF WINTER, IN THE DARK AND WITH A GALE BLOWING.

Supertanker Puzzle Bonus Question: when the supertanker does hit a rock, how much marine life will die?

With the gutting of environmental protection regulations, Canada is becoming a polluter's safe haven.

We also have Asian-made bikes to ride in our bike lanes.

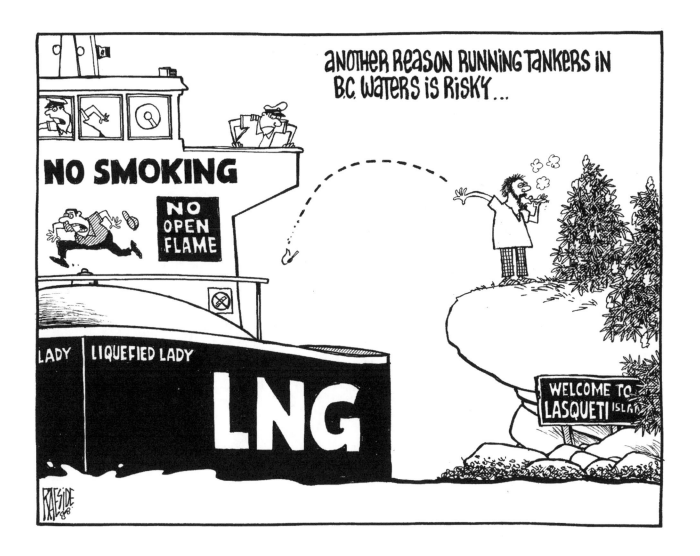

Besides the obvious geological hazards, there are other unique dangers that must be considered when transporting liquid natural gas along the BC coast.

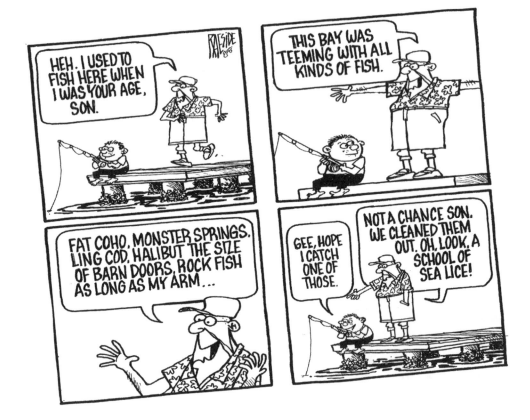

WE SHOOT IT, trap it, net it, wipe out its nests, choke off its food supply, kick it out of its natural habitat and run over it. Yet we're puzzled when the salmon don't return, horrified when starving cougars prey on small children, and annoyed when bears go through the trash cans that replaced their berry patch. The government spends millions of dollars on advertising to lure tourists to experience BC's wildlife, while at the same time inviting trophy hunters to come and shoot it. One assumes that if we run out of wildlife the government will sell licences to shoot tourists.

The government floated the idea of building wilderness lodges within BC parks.

Of course, this wouldn't happen if the staff was paid a decent wage.

The Department of Fisheries and Oceans' calculations of the number of returning BC salmon isn't an art. It's a joke.

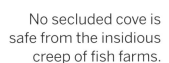

No secluded cove is safe from the insidious creep of fish farms.

Fortunately, Barry was not shot by police or conservation officers. He was run over by a minivan.

THE DOWN-SIDE TO EAGLE NEST CAMS:

EDDIE THE EAGLE WAS HATCHED LIVE, IN FRONT OF MILLIONS OF WEB VIEWERS...

HIS FAME GREW. TALK SHOWS, BOOK DEALS, PARTS ON SITCOMS...

AND THEN, CONAN, I SAID TO MADONNA: SORRY, I'M DOING THE BRITNEY VIDEO!

HAH! HAH! HAH!

GIRLS, FAST CARS, EDDIE HAD IT ALL. BUT THEN, THE SUBSTANCE ABUSE STARTED...

WITHIN A YEAR, THE PHONE STOPPED RINGING AND EDDIE WAS REDUCED TO SELLING HIS TAIL FEATHERS FOR BOOZE...

NOW EDDIE IS LIVING IN AN ALLEY OFF HOLLYWOOD BLVD.

HEY, WEREN'T YOU ON 'EIGHT IS ENOUGH?'

Everyone loves the eagle webcams, but where is the support after they fly the nest?

45

Next: reservations for wild salmon.

The operator of an illegal marijuana plantation was found to have a guard bear.

BC farmers—fed up with deer munching through their crops—sometimes resort to desperate measures in order to cull the invading herds.

WILDLIFE MANAGEMENT, B.C.-STYLE:

SHOOT THE WOLVES, BECAUSE THEY'RE PREYING ON GAME ANIMALS, LIKE DEER.

SHOOT THE DEER, AS THEIR POPULATION IS EXPLODING DUE TO THE LACK OF PREDATORS- LIKE WOLVES.

SHOOT THE COUGARS. WITH NO DEER TO PREY ON, THEY'RE STARVING AND MOVING INTO URBAN AREAS IN SEARCH OF FOOD.

SHOOT THE BEARS. WITH THE WOLVES AND COUGARS GONE WE CAN BUILD HOMES IN WHAT WAS ONCE WILDERNESS AND IT'S A NUISANCE TO HAVE TO SECURE BEAR ATTRACTANTS LIKE HOUSEHOLD GARBAGE.

This is what happens when you have an endless supply of ammunition and an endless lack of brains.

The frequency of automobile incidents involving wildlife increases as the animals become more urbanized...

...incidents which will only get worse if a bridge is ever built across the Georgia Strait.

We seem to care more about the edible, tastier wildlife.

As we encroach on their habitat, wildlife is forced to adapt.

How often do we hear the phrase "we had no choice but to destroy it"?

And if a conservation officer doesn't shoot it, someone else will.

For the small percentage of "problem" wildlife that does get relocated: a lifetime of drug dependency.

RESOURCES

BC IS a RESOURCE-BASED PROVINCE and everything that grows or lurks underground is worth something to someone. From trees to gas, someone is prepared to pay the government a licence fee to get what they want. Logging practices have barely left enough old-growth Douglas fir to manufacture a year's supply of toothpicks for a mid-sized restaurant. Then consider the punitive duties on BC softwood lumber and raw log exports and, suddenly, those who once worked in the woods are now working in that restaurant. With so little of our forests left to exploit, even environmental groups who once fought epic battles with the forest companies are now reduced to saving the occasional Garry oak tree. LNG plants are supposed to be the latest resource to drive jobs but, so far, none have been built—and if they are built they will probably be constructed by cheap foreign labour.

BC's forests disappear faster than campaign promises the day after an election.

The 1993 protests over old-growth logging in Clayoquot Sound eventually moved to the steps of the BC Legislature.

As the protests grew to become the largest act of civil disobedience the province had ever seen, then NDP premier Mike Harcourt tried to mollify protestors, while saving forestry jobs.

Not that there were many forestry jobs left to save in BC.

US lumber companies, backed up by the US Commerce Department, were relentless in trying to put BC lumber producers out of business through crippling tariffs.

When the tariffs were finally overturned, the industry was hit with quotas.

Flush with cash from all the crap we buy from them, China came calling.

The government was more concerned with stopping British Columbians from smoking than keeping lumber mills open.

Mind you, the Europeans wiped out their forests decades ago—you'd think we might have learned something.

The mountain pine beetle—destroyer of lodgepole pine forests—has impacted BC's forestry industry and continues its devastation in an unprecedented epidemic...

...but what will happen when the beetles run out of trees?

Like so many other sectors of the economy, the promise for a solution to something already broken only arises at election time.

NOTWITHSTANDING A FEW BRIEF PERIODS when there were three provincial parties, British Columbia is usually a two-party province, which—for those few of us who bother turning up to vote—does simplify the ballot come election time. We now have a Green Party MLA in the Legislature, which lends a certain air of civility to the building, but it won't be long before Question Period reverts back to the same kind of behaviour one would encounter at an Asian cockfight.

In 1997, British Columbia's brief experiment with the Reform Party ended.

Glen Clark's New Democratic Party (NDP) absorbed Gordon Wilson's short-lived Progressive Democratic Alliance (PDA)—and its debt.

In 2001, then premier Gordon Campbell began his decade-long leadership with "Team Liberal."

It wasn't long before the polls tanked and Team Liberal got the knives out.

In a rare show of unity, both the Liberal and New Democratic parties agreed to keep their MLA expenses hidden from those who pay their bills...

...although taxpayers weren't getting much bang for their buck.

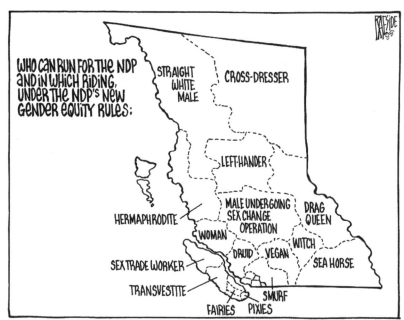

New NDP leader Carole James introduced gender equity for prospective candidates in an upcoming election...

...and piously refused to let her caucus take the scheduled salary raise.

After a brief but ugly battle in 2010, Carole James stepped down when it became clear that several caucus members opposed her continued leadership.

And the NDP started rebuilding. Again.

Adrian Dix decided to take the NDP party in a new direction—not that everyone wanted to follow him...

...but with Christy Clark's Liberals tanking in the polls how could he lose?

As the B.C. Liberals continue their slide in the polls, some senior government members polish their resignation speeches:

Draft #1

Holy smokes! Have you seen our poll numbers? The ebola virus is more popular than we are! We're doomed, doomed, I tell you! And I'm not sticking around to see this train wreck, I'm getting the heck out of here.

Of course, it has been an honour to have served the people, etc, etc.

Draft #2

Last night I saw a police car parked outside the Legislature. It could have been nothing, perhaps just responding to a domestic disturbance across the street... Anyhoo, I've decided to leave office and move into a cave. Do not try to contact me.

It has been a privilege to serve, etc.

Draft #3

Look, I didn't vote for Christy and I didn't vote for Gordo. Heck, I didn't know I was a member of the Liberal Party until today! I'm as shocked as I'm sure you are and will tender my resignation immediately after receiving my last paycheque.

Oh, and thanks for the fat pension!

Final draft

It has been a privilege and an honour to have had the opportunity to serve the people of this wonderful province. Although I would dearly love to stay on and fight the next election, I have decided to resign, in order to be able to spend more time with my pet iguana, Larry.

RAESIDE

Liberal party members trampled over each other to get to the exit. Of course, the impending train wreck had nothing to do with it.

Green Party leader Elizabeth May: the Energizer Bunny of politics.

John Cummins' Conservative Party—which began by sucking disaffected Liberals into its fold—ended up just sucking.

GOVERNMENT IS EVERYWHERE. Not just in the Legislature, but also in the guise of Crown corporations like BC Hydro, ICBC, or municipalities that treat our homes as ATMs. To serve us better, our government hires "the best and brightest minds" and then raises our taxes to pay their salaries. And when those "brightest minds" turn out to be not so bright and end up getting turfed, the government raises our taxes to pay their severance packages.

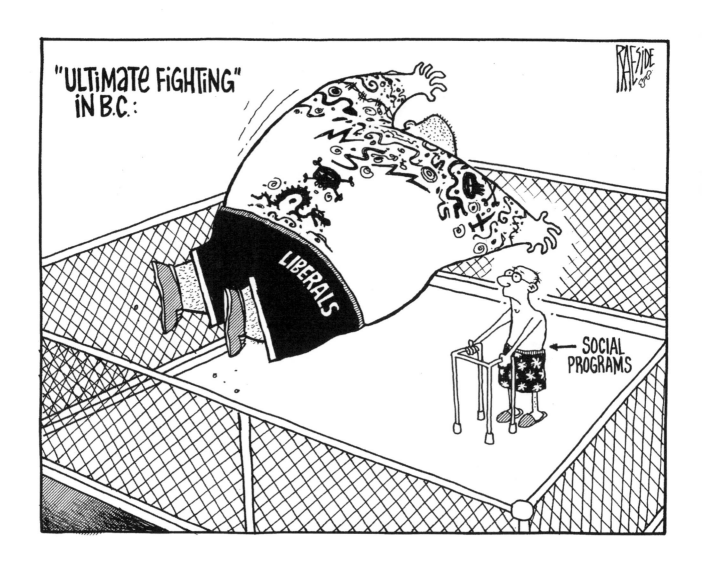

Ultimate Fighting arrived in BC, to the disgust of some... but we've had different forms of Ultimate Fighting in BC for decades.

BC's Ministry of Children and Families was in a perpetual state of crisis.

It turned out that there was an expiry date on children who were under its care.

We think of our home as our castle. Municipalities think of it as their piggy bank.

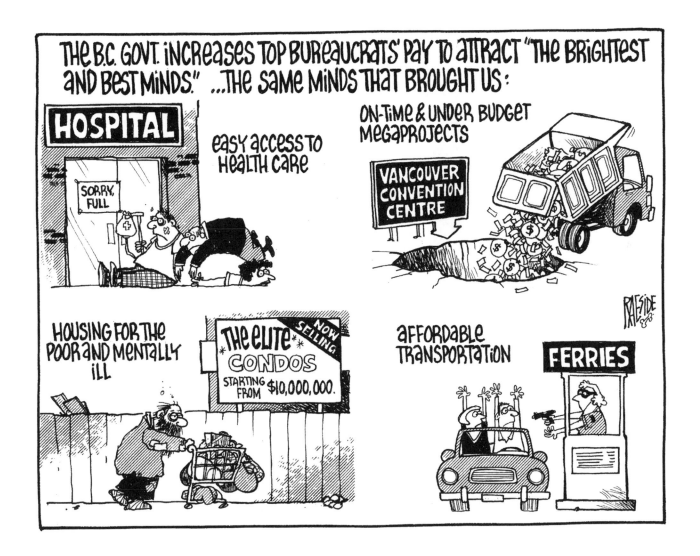

The "brightest and best minds" are hired by government to come up with more novel ways to screw us.

UPPER MANAGEMENT GET DROPPED FROM GOVERNMENT:

CUSHY CONSULTING CONTRACTS

SEVERANCE $

AUXILIARIES, CLERKS, & OTHER MINIONS GET DROPPED FROM GOVERNMENT:

And when those "brightest and best minds" leave government we pay for them again.

Liberal MLA Kevin Krueger, who had a reputation for being "outspoken," left the caucus.

A KRUEGER HAS BEEN SIGHTED IN THE DOWNTOWN CORE. CONSERVATION OFFICERS WARN B.C. CONSERVATIVE PARTY OFFICIALS TO KEEP MEMBERS INDOORS UNTIL HE CAN BE TRACKED, TRANQUILIZED AND RETURNED TO THE LEGISLATURE.

BREAKING NEWS · KRUEGER SIGHTING IN

It turns out that under the watch of the "brightest and best minds," the Legislature accounts were in a shambles with millions of dollars being unaccounted for.

However, if you give your position as "Rideau Canal, Ottawa" you may be saved in a matter of seconds.

It didn't take much to earn a bonus if you worked for the Insurance Corporation of British Columbia...

...especially if you can figure out ingenious ways to pay for those bonuses.

With the high cost of living in BC, there are a lot of families who can't afford to take a holiday—particularly if they have to find childcare on a holiday in order to get to their minimum-wage job.

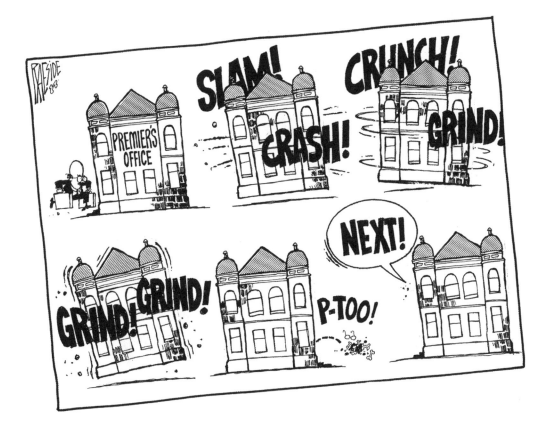

BC HAS BEEN BLESSED with a long line of colourful characters in the Office of the Premier. We've had drunks, theme park owners, high school dropouts, trailer park managers and union organizers. They all enter office with high hopes and—one assumes—the best of intentions. But as their term progresses, the rot sets in, the polls tank and caucus turns ugly. While the electorate salivates at the prospect of delivering the coup de grâce, it's usually their own party that quietly removes them from the premier's office wrapped in a rug. It's another quaint BC tradition...

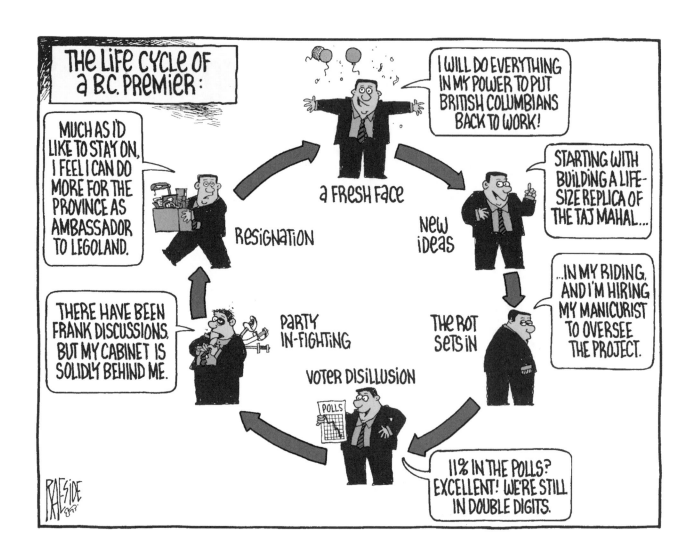

Similar to the life cycle of a moth.

From 1986-91, Social Credit premier Bill Vander Zalm and his mouth arced across BC like a comet...

...and like all comets he eventually crashed and burned.

The Zalm would one day rise again. And again. And again.

...but his successor, Rita Johnston, put the Socred Party out of its misery.

The Clayoquot Sound logging protests dominated NDP premier Mike Harcourt's time in office...

...along with various other scandals.

After sticking the shiv into Harcourt, Glen Clark took the reins of the NDP government and fast-tracked the First Nations' land claims process.

It turned out that the NDP's pre-election budget numbers were mostly BS.

Clark's woes were piling up: the Fast Ferry fiasco, gaming licences, suspicious decks...

...but it was gaming licences that finally did Clark in.

Ujjal Dosanjh inherited the NDP and was subsequently turfed in the next election. But after a miraculous change of philosophy, he was back as a Liberal MP.

The Gordon Campbell Liberals took over government, and immediately began privatizing assets—until they got to privatizing the Coquihalla Highway, where the wheels fell off and the honeymoon ended.

Campbell snivelled for forgiveness after getting arrested for drunk driving in Maui.

After the sale of BC Rail to CN, no public asset was safe.

With the NDP gaining traction in the polls, Campbell suddenly embraced everything green.

Christy "Photo-Op" Clark takes over the Liberal Party, the airwaves and our tax dollars.

BRITISH COLUMBIANS DON'T ELECT GOVERNMENTS. We throw the old one out and hope vaguely the new one will make less of a mess of things. No pollster can accurately predict the mood of the electorate, as we like to keep our "options open," which is really just another way of saying we can't stand any of them. If anyone named None of the Above ever runs for public office, they'll win by a landslide.

In BC we change our minds more often than we change our underwear.

Premier Ujjal Dosanjh called an election that everyone already knew the outcome of.

New Liberal premier Gordon Campbell cleaned out social programs, while party hacks and MLAs who lost the election cleaned up.

Social programs are always paroled from the budget-cuts dungeon, just prior to the next election.

The Single Transferable Vote (STV) was more confusing than the assembly instructions for a BBQ. Besides, any ballot that required more than one "X" was doomed to failure.

Gordon Campbell's re-election campaign was carefully planned to avoid the issues...

...while Carole James' campaign just kept running into them.

Finally, BC had an Official Opposition again.

NDP leader Adrian Dix finally went negative-ish.

The BC Liberals could elect a new leader—as long as they had a PIN number.

Some British Columbians tend to think of voting as a bother when, in fact, it's a duty.

To the victor go the spoils.

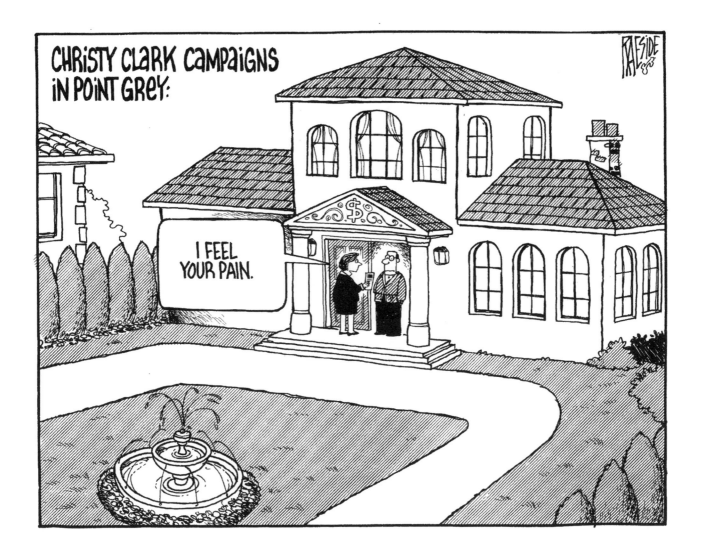

New Liberal Party leader Christy Clark campaigned tirelessly for the 1 percent.

Summer elections distract us from beach duty. Winter elections interrupt our ski trips.

YEARS FROM NOW, the Liberal government's introduction of the Harmonized Sales Tax (HST) will be presented to Political Science students as the most bungled, poorly thought-out idea since New Coke. Assuming the electorate was distracted by the warm glow of another four years with him as BC's premier, Gordon Campbell announced the HST but was unprepared for the backlash. His government sent out MLAs and a bunch of badly drawn stick figures to sell the tax—but it would have been easier selling plague rats. At the end of the day the tax was defeated in a province-wide referendum, and Campbell was exiled to the Consulate-General's office in London, where he survives with only one chauffeur.

The HST was introduced in 2010—at the same time we paid our property taxes. Bad timing is everything.

Prior to the election, Campbell said the Liberals had no intention of introducing the HST—although nobody believed him, especially restaurateurs, who saw an immediate drop in business.

Almost immediately, government MLAs were feeling the backlash from their constituents, who were starting petitions to scrap the tax.

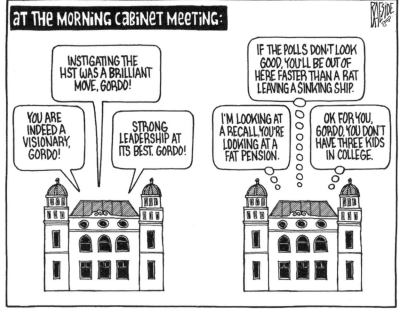

Backed into a corner by growing outrage—and the growing petition—the government scrambled to feebly justify the HST.

The anti-HST petition gained traction with the efforts of Bill Vander Zalm, who returned to the political spotlight to fight the tax.

For those tasked with selling the tax it was an uphill battle.

Truckloads of our tax dollars were poured into promoting the HST.

The government tried linking the HST to better health care.

Although they would benefit most from the HST, BC business was reluctant to get into the dogfight.

When Christy Clark became premier, she inherited the HST.

The results of the referendum were clear and the province's experiment with the HST was obliterated in the hurricane...

...along with Gordon Campbell's legacy as premier.

It was hard to know what was worse: the HST, or the creepy stick figures used to sell it.

THE GOOD NEWS is that BC residents are living longer than ever before. The bad news is that BC residents are living longer than ever before. We have a health care system originally designed to treat teenagers with a bad case of acne—not octogenarians with decaying hips. This tsunami of grey is spilling out of acute care wards and into the hallways of hospitals. Health authority executives respond by raising their salaries, the nurses union by threatening to walk off the job, and the government by building bigger hallways.

Those who feared BC was moving to a two-tiered health care system ignored the fact that we already had a two-tiered everything else.

With hospital emergency rooms overflowing, wait times stretched into hours...

...and with the latest government plan, hours could turn into days.

Regardless of how much money was thrown at health care, it never seemed to go to where it was most needed.

To move patients through the system faster, health authorities came up with incentives.

Patients were finally moved out of hallways.

The endless health unions/health ministry bargaining only hurt one group, and it wasn't either of them.

Reluctantly, government allowed private clinics to set up shop.

Health forums proved as effective as leeches, but leeches cost less.

Gambling brings in revenue. Sick people do not...

...or do they?

At which time it will be rescheduled to Stardate 4539.

YOU Can'T GO FaR in this province without encountering a bait car, bait bike, bait snowmobile or even bait skis. And if you do decide to take a ride in a bait car, chances are you'll be caught and perhaps tasered. And chances are there will be someone with a cellphone camera who will record the incident and put it up on YouTube. It's no wonder we're called "Hollywood North."

Police routinely take to the air to look for pot plantations hidden in the woods.
Not that they ever have to look that hard.

WHAT IF THE GOVT. PLAN TO FREE UP THE COURTS BY ALLOWING TRAFFIC TICKETS TO BE DISPUTED BY PHONE WAS EXPANDED...

DUDE, THERE'S NO WAY I WAS DOING 260K IN A SCHOOL ZONE. MY FERRARI ONLY DOES 240.

...TO MORE SERIOUS CRIMES:

YES, THAT'S RIGHT, MY HUSBAND FELL DOWN THE STAIRS... NO, I CAN DISPOSE OF THE BODY.

If you're being murdered, press #1. If you're the murderer, press #2.

...AND IF CASES ACTUALLY DID GET TO COURT:

WELL, JUDGING BY HIS PHOTO, I'D SAY HE'S GUILTY, YOUR HONOUR.

BUT HE DOES HAVE NICE EYES.

COULD THIS EVEN BE EXTENDED TO COVER MATTERS OF PUBLIC POLICY?

HELLO, CHRISTY? I VOTE FOR FEB 13 FOR FAMILY DAY, AND DON'T WEAR THOSE RED PUMPS WITH THAT CHANEL SUIT.

CHIEF, THE BAIT CAR PROGRAM IS A HUGE SUCCESS! JUST THE THOUGHT THAT A CAR COULD BE RIGGED, IS DETERRING THIEVES FROM STEALING FAMILY CARS.

...THEY'RE STEALING POLICE CARS, INSTEAD.

To curb an epidemic of car thefts, BC police forces introduced bait cars... then bait bikes, bait snowmobiles, bait donuts, bait recycling boxes, etcetera.

WHAT OTHER UNKNOWN EXPENDITURES COULD BE HIDDEN IN THE NEW RCMP CONTRACT?

Municipalities had to sign the new province-wide RCMP contract without knowing what was inside.

New drunk-driving laws and quickie roadside convictions make a night out stressful, not only for patrons, but also for restaurant owners.

And those unfortunate enough to be caught up in the new drunk-driving laws had to install a driver interlock device...

...but why stop at motorists who've had a few drinks?

In response to a rash of complaints about police misconduct, The Office of the Police Complaint Commissioner was set up...

... to review the inevitable barrage of citizen cellphone videos of questionable police tactics.

Police were overwhelmed by the size of the protest at the 1997 Asia-Pacific Economic Cooperation (APEC) meeting in Vancouver and almost ran out of pepper spray.

A police dog is accused of using excessive force in taking down a suspect. Suspended for two weeks with biscuits?

Even low-lifes have rights.

Nabbing a drunk driver was one thing. Catching a driver who was stoned was another.

Introduced by the NDP in the '90s, the short-lived photo radar program was considered just another sneaky tax on motorists. And witches.

Even though BC cities are littered with bait cars, there are still idiots out there who will steal them.

VICTORIA HAS LIVED off its olde-worlde charm for decades and Oak Bay hasn't changed much since the Paleolithic period. Part of the reason Vancouver Island is so unique is thanks to the masterminds at the BC Ferry Corporation, who stay awake at night coming up with new ways to raise fares and cut routes. But once you sell a kidney to pay the ferry fare, you can marvel at Victoria's pop-up urinals, electric scooter traffic jams and the construction of Victoria's sewer—which is taking longer to build than the Great Pyramids.

The mad dash to catch a ferry to the mainland was somewhat eased by electronic highway signs indicating how full the ferry is and which sailing has been cancelled due to a "mechanical malfunction."

The brightest minds at the BC Ferry Corporation just can't seem to figure out why ridership is down.

Mr. Floatie, a gentleman dressed as a giant turd, turned up at regular intervals to protest Greater Victoria discharging raw sewage into the ocean.

The search for new uses for the island railroad coincided with the explosion of the rabbit population at University of Victoria.

The Victoria Police Department (gently) grapples with octogenarian criminals.

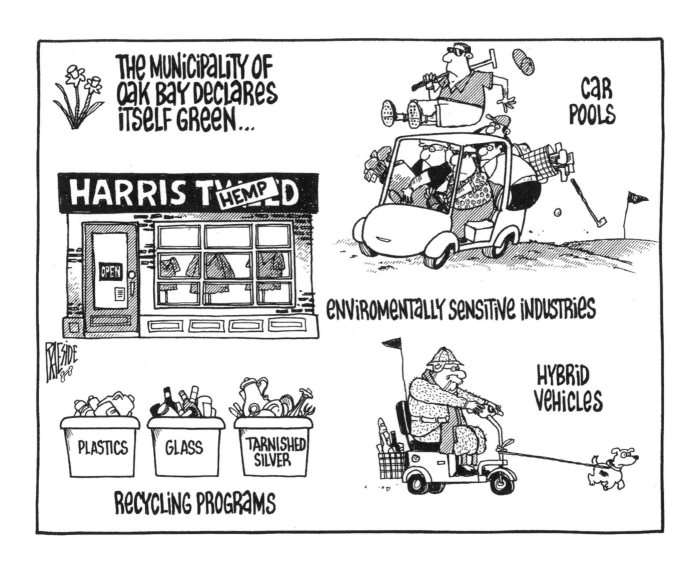

Oak Bay—a community with no industry and no gas station—proudly declares itself "green."

Rather than go to the expense of installing snow tires, Victoria drivers prefer to use solid objects to stop their vehicles.

This is easily the most-used phrase during the "Wet Coast" winter.

There are those on the Island who refuse to acknowledge that winter will occasionally put in a brief appearance.

Or, perhaps it was a deer suicide by motorized scooter.

Tofino's water reservoir dried up at the height of tourist season.

Following the earthquake and tsunami in Japan, there are fears that radiation from the crippled nuclear power plant could hit the BC coast—before the first oil tanker does.

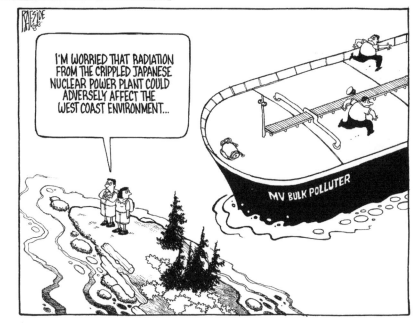

Every windstorm brings out the usual windsurfers who play chicken with Mother Nature.

Biologists collected the remains of a humpback whale that washed up on the beach. In lieu of flowers, a donation to the Krill Research Foundation is appreciated.

Those who were working to save the endangered Vancouver Island marmot resorted to desperate measures. But was Squeaky really single?

A quake and subsequent tsunami alert panicked some Island residents who fled to higher ground.

The annual poke in the nose to everyone back East is often in the middle of our rainy season. But at least we don't have to shovel it.

In the wake of the 911 terrorist attacks, there were fears that float planes could be used as terrorist weapons.

Victoria Parking Commissionaires felt that they can do more than just harass motorists.

Voracious American bullfrogs took over Elk Lake, threatening native frogs and shaking them down for their fly money.

Engineers warn that Victoria's iconic Legislature dome could collapse during an earthquake, meaning it would have to be replaced by another iconic structure.

Officials worry about the quality of the water we drink but don't seem to be concerned about the quality of the water others have to live in.

Not to mention the cost of the trowel and the six-month training course on how to use it.

Defence Department officials in the nation's capital think that they can run the Pacific fleet from Ottawa, even though they don't know where the Pacific is.

LIKE EVERY RECENT OLYMPICS, the organizers assured taxpayers they would come in under the initial budget, there would be no disruption to our lives and that hosting the games would bring a huge economic boom. And like every recent Olympics, they didn't. All the 2010 Winter Olympics brought was hordes of cops from across the country tasked with guarding metal security fences (it must have worked, none were stolen), traffic chaos, confusion, draconian trademark punishments and colossal expenditures. In fact, we had everything except snow—which shouldn't have been a huge surprise since Vancouver is in a rainforest.

The Olympic party started early, for some...

...followed by the cost overruns.

THE OLYMPIC RELAY

Attending the 2010 games was beginning to sound about as much fun as spending two weeks in a Stalinist gulag.

THE FOLLOWING ARE THE ONLY WORDS IN THE ENGLISH LANGUAGE NOT TRADEMARKED BY VANOC:

SOARING CONSTRUCTION COSTS, BUDGET SHORTFALL, SOCIAL HOUSING, UNDERESTIMATED SECURITY COSTS, HOTEL ROOM SHORTAGE, DOWNTOWN EAST SIDE, BUDGET OVERSIGHT, ACCOUNTABILITY, EAGLERIDGE BLUFFS, PROTESTING GRANDMOTHERS, HOMELESS SHELTERS, GRIZZLY BEAR HABITAT AND TAXPAYER-FUNDED.

The Vancouver Organizing Committee for the 2010 Olympic and Paralympic Winter Games (VANOC) sent its goons out to punish anyone using words even slightly related to the Olympics.

With all the visitors expected, some Vancouver hotel owners found ways to accommodate.

Meanwhile, the rest of the province had its own Olympics.

As the games become increasingly commercialized, hosting the Olympics has become a bizarre undertaking—to the point that there is no longer anything dignified about them.

Organizers explained that it costs money to be "world class"—but then, it wasn't their money.

The Canadian team uniforms looked like they were designed by committee—a very drunk committee.

The Feds were building their own pavilion but the contents were a closely guarded secret.

VANOC had everything in hand—except snow.

2010 OLYMPIC PINS

COLLECT 'EM ALL!

SURVEILLANCE CAMERA PIN

SNOWFLAKE PIN (VERY RARE)

TRUCKING SNOW TO CYPRESS MOUNTAIN PIN

EMISSIONS FROM ALL THE TRUCKS, BUSES, VANOC VEHICLES AND GENERATORS PIN

PERSON WHO CAME UP WITH THE IDEA OF HOLDING WINTER SPORTS IN A RAINFOREST PIN

?

WHAT IT'S ALL GOING TO COST PIN

Pin collecting and trading is a traditional pastime during the Olympics although, sadly, none of these pins were available.

WE'RE NOT CONCERNED IF CYPRESS MOUNTAIN DOESN'T GET ENOUGH SNOW. WE HAVE THE ABILITY TO MAKE ARTIFICIAL SNOW. BUT WE ALSO HAVE A BACKUP PLAN...

WE CAN STOCKPILE SNOW AT HIGHER ELEVATIONS, BUT WE HAVE ANOTHER BACKUP PLAN...

VANOC puts its "holy crap, we don't have any fricking snow" backup plan into gear.

WE CAN SPREAD HAY OVER THE SNOW TO INSULATE IT, BUT WE HAVE ANOTHER BACKUP PLAN...

FORGET THE TORCH. FROM HERE ON, YOU'LL BE RUNNING TO VANCOUVER WITH SHOVELS FULL OF SNOW.

GOLDEN

The snow eventually turned up but sometimes the spectators didn't.

Whistler—usually in a cannabis haze—could be a problem for athletes who, of course, never touch the stuff.

The obsession with getting gold sometimes overshadowed the spirit of competition.

The "Olympic experience" was available to anyone, even outside of the actual venues.

Some folks never got over their brief moment basking in the glow of the Olympic cauldron.

FOREST FIRES, MUDSLIDES, FLOODS, EARTHQUAKES... BC has 'em all. Every small quake brings out the usual warnings from the Provincial Emergency folks that we're overdue for "The Big One" and we'd better be prepared. The more cautious people rush out and buy an emergency kit and the rest of us make a mental note of where they hide it. Elected officials assure us they're ready to respond but if the quake strikes they will in fact be useless—the Legislature dome will have collapsed and they will all be dead.

Fortunately, there are some folks who are prepared for a natural disaster in BC.

Hopefully, seismic upgrading of BC schools will move faster than the tectonic plates are moving.

Many British Columbians are not prepared for "the big one"...

...however, some are.

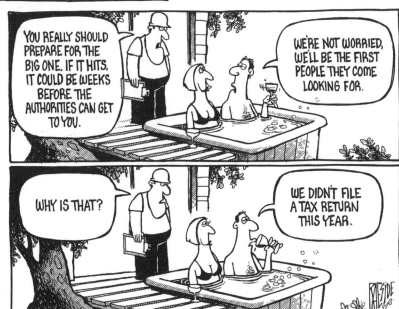

Thousands of hectares of denuded BC hillsides have become a ticking time bomb.

Despite regular flooding, life in the Fraser Valley goes on.

There are those who like to watch firefighting operations...

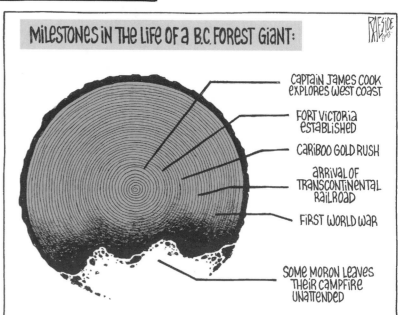

... and those who start them.

In the aftermath of the Japanese tsunami, the BC government was rethinking its emergency plans.

Debris that washed up on our shores from the tsunami has turned out to be much less than the garbage we throw into the ocean on a daily basis.

After a major disaster, we're told to be prepared to survive on our own for at least 72 hours...

...but there is such a thing as over-preparedness.

Despite dire warnings over rising sea levels, the price of waterfront property is still at a premium.

Every minor quake is an excuse for major housecleaning.

BRITISH COLUMBIA: where else can you ski in the morning, garden in the afternoon and, in the evening, phone relatives back east to rub it in?